A FRIENDSHIP STORY

HEART & MIND

Written by Nishi Singhal
Creator of the Heart & Mind Series

Illustrated by Lera Munoz

PRECOCITY PRESS

Sign up here for a free Joy Journal for kids!
To help them further create a partnership between their
hearts and minds. www.joyparade.co/freebie

Editor: Lorraine Wadman
Creative Director and Designer: Susan Shankin
Illustrator: Lera Munoz

ISBN: 978-1-7373539-7-3

Library of Congress Control Number: 2020911581

Published by Precocity Press
Venice, CA 90291

First edition. Printed and bound in the United States of America

Heart and Mind are the very best of friends
and have been all their lives.

They each have their own special qualities
and keep each other balanced.

1

Mind is great at learning and solving problems.

Mind knows that if you tie your shoelaces,
you will not trip and fall on them.

Mind is also great at taking action.

If Mind wanted to make banana bread,
it would start by taking out the ingredients.

HEART TALKS TO US THROUGH JOY & LOVE

Heart is amazing at loving you.

It doesn't matter if you trip and fall on your shoelaces
or burn the banana bread,
Heart loves YOU exactly the way you are.

Heart is great at being in the HERE and NOW.

This means Heart doesn't worry
about yesterday or tomorrow.

When you follow your heart,
you feel joy in the HERE and NOW.

If Heart feels the spark to dance,
but Mind thinks that it will look silly
since it is not a REAL dancer...

Heart can tell Mind that it will love
without any judgment.

Mind is always ready to take action if Heart
is having a hard time knowing what it wants.

Mind will hold Heart's hand and take one step in
any direction until they know what Heart wants.

When Heart and Mind work together,
life feels fun and easier.

One day, Heart and Mind decided
to spend the day apart.

Heart wanted to lie in the grass
and watch the clouds passing by.

Mind thought this was too boring and
decided to find something else to do.

Mind kept thinking and thinking

and walking and walking.

Mind thought about
going swimming, then Mind
thought about how it wasn't a great swimmer,
then Mind thought about how it should really
take swimming lessons, then Mind thought about
whether to take swimming lessons at the pool or
at the lake, then Mind thought about . . .

Mind kept thinking until the sun started to set.

"Oh no, it's time for me to go home.
But I didn't get to do anything fun!"

"Hi, Mind!"

"Oh, hi Heart"

"It looks like you had a lovely walk today!"

"What do you mean?"

"I was on top of that big hill, and I
could see you walking around the grassy field.
It looked like a lot of fun!"

"I wasn't able to enjoy it.
I was too busy thinking about
what I should be doing with my day."

13

Heart smiled.

"Remember what I always say:
Enjoy where you are right now. Because right now is your
greatest gift. That's why we call it The Present."

"Did you enjoy watching the clouds pass by?"

"I did! But soon after you left,
I felt like going for a swim. So I went to the lake.
When I got there, Ms. Lifeguard was
teaching a swimming class, so I joined.
After the class, I decided to watch the sunset!"

"Whoa. You did a lot today. You had a busy day."

"I had a FUN day because I followed my joy.
But I felt like you were with me every step of the way."

"When I felt the spark of what to do next.
I asked myself: What would Mind do?
since you are amazing at taking action."

"That's why we are best friends.
I help you focus on what you enjoy in the present,
and you help me take action."

ideas

Learning

inspiration

creating

action

17

JOY
LOVE JOY

Mind thought about it for a second
and suddenly saw the night sky above.

"Hey, wouldn't it be fun to lie in the grass
and look for shooting stars?"

Heart and Mind lay in the grass watching the stars.
And whenever Mind started to think too much, Heart
reminded Mind of the joy of being in the present.

That's what friends are for.

DISCUSSION QUESTIONS

☆ What have you learned through your mind? How to tell time? How to measure ingredients for baking a cake? The names of your classmates?

☆ What types of action does your mind like to take? Does it like to write? Swim? Run? Play the piano?

☆ How does your heart show you love? The next time your mind judges you for making a mistake, like misspelling a word, allow your heart to love you.

☆ What does it mean to be in the HERE and NOW? Are you planning what to do after dinner? Are you thinking about what your friend said to you at school?

☆ How does it feel when you are in the HERE and NOW? Do you feel more joy and love? Peaceful and calm?

☆ Has your mind ever kept thinking and thinking, and you wished you could turn it off? What did you do to turn it off?

☆ Do you think Heart and Mind are good partners? Why?

EXERCISES

KEEPING HEART & MIND BALANCED

Practice listening to your heart and use your mind to take action.

☆ Close your eyes.

☆ Take some deep breaths.

☆ Let thoughts and mental pictures pass by.

☆ Allow yourself to relax.

☆ Ask your heart, "What do you want to do right now?

☆ Wait and listen for a response.

☆ Use your mind to take action.

Ideas from your heart can come through as words, images, feelings, or a joyful burst of action!

LIVE IN THE HERE & NOW

Practice living in the present. Start with exercise above. If your mind wanders into thinking about yesterday and tomorrow, come back into the present.

☆ Be a lion! Take a deep breath in through your nose, open your mouth, and roar the air out.

☆ Place one hand on your heart and the other hand on your belly, close your eyes, and stare into the blackness.

☆ Pick a color! Look around and find everything you can that is that color.

☆ Pet your dog or cuddle a favorite stuffed animal!

Hello, Caregivers!

Thank you for choosing to share this book with your little ones and yourself! The more present we can become, the more we increase our capacity for joy.

I wrote this book for young people to understand that they are not their minds. They have a mind that can perform a variety of tasks but ultimately, they exist beyond it. When the mind can be viewed as a tool available to us, we can then view moments of anxious thinking as the overuse of this one tool.

Along with overthinking, over-doing becomes a deterrent from being present in the moment. Believing that we are not complete without checking off the endless to-do list becomes conditioned within us if we do not accept that we are unconditionally loved right now. This book helps to teach young ones that regardless of what they do or do not do, they are complete, whole, and loved right now.

I hope you and your loved ones have enjoyed this first book in my Heart & Mind series! These books are meant to remind us how to live joyfully through the tools we already have inside us.

Love,
Nishi

ABOUT THE AUTHOR

NISHI SINGHAL has a bachelor's degree in psychology from the University of Michigan and a master's degree in public health from the University of Illinois at Chicago. Nishi is a public health expert, an integrated consciousness coach, and certified yoga teacher. Nishi has studied psychology, consciousness, and neuroscience with Joe Dispenza, Eckhart Tolle, and Deepak Chopra. She has worked with various nonprofits on bettering communities and currently serves as The Lively Community Foundation's director.

Inspired by her work with children through teaching yoga, Nishi created Joy Parade, an online space dedicated to teaching children and their caretakers how to bring presence into their day-to-day living. Nishi wrote *A Friendship Story: Heart & Mind* to introduce the concept of presence so that anyone (big or small) can live a more balanced and joyful life. Nishi's mission is to create light and fun ways for young people to view life through writing and one-on-one coaching.

Visit **JoyParade.co** to learn more and for additional resources.

ABOUT THE ILLUSTRATOR

LERA MUNOZ is an illustrator specializing in children's illustration. She loves to create playful characters and imaginary worlds that inspire young minds. Her work is perfect for storytelling and has been described as charming and full of warmth.

Lera lives in France with her husband and 4-year-old daughter. Being from Russia and now living in France, Lera takes the best from both cultures. In her free time, she likes to read, meditate, and travel. Her life is filled with domestic warmth and smiles of family and friends. For more information, visit leramunoz.com.

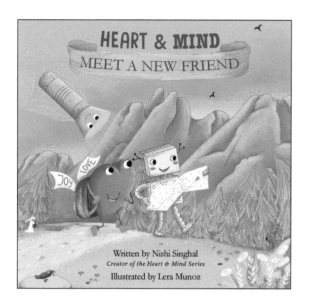

HEART & MIND: MEET A NEW FRIEND

The two friends are back! This time Heart & Mind meet a new friend, Awareness, a superhero flashlight who teaches them how to release heavy emotions like anger, sadness, and fear. Read along as your child develops new skills of letting their emotions pass like clouds in the sky so that they can live a more joyous life!

TESTIMONIALS

Heart, mind, and awareness are critical for the wellness and success of everyone's life, children and adults alike. This beautiful book brings insightful awareness to this important topic.

~Dr. Rulin Xiu, Quantum Physicist, founder of Tao Science and Authorr

This book is a great way to teach kids the power of managing their emotions and how different parts of them can work together to do so. It is very well written and the illustrations are darling!

~Analisa Jayasekera, Licensed Marriage and Family Therapist

Children all over the world will be overjoyed to meet their new friend. As they grow, getting to know their own characters and embracing more of themselves through story, their new friend(s) will go very far in helping them to feel comforted, reassured, and able to interpret the many thoughts and emotions they have to deal with each and every day. Brilliantly illustrated, friendly, and emotionally moving, you will enjoy sharing with your kiddos about their friends and how to live a balanced life with presence and focus.

~Kelly Pierce, Certified Life & Business Coach, Reiki Master, and RTT Practitioner

CPSIA information can be obtained
at www.ICGtesting.com
Printed in the USA
BVHW021954190821
614611BV00035B/1228

HEART & MIND
MEET A NEW FRIEND

Written by Nishi Singhal

Creator of the Heart & Mind Series

Illustrated by Lera Munoz

PRECOCITY PRESS

Editor: Lorraine Wadman
Creative Director and Designer: Susan Shankin
Illustrator: Lera Munoz

ISBN: 978-1-7373539-2-8

Library of Congress Control Number: 2021913217

Published by Precocity Press
Venice, CA 90291

First edition. Printed and bound in the United States of America

Heart and Mind are the very best of friends
and have been all their lives.

Today, they are spending the day
with Awareness, a new friend.

Awareness helps Mind focus on taking action
and learning new things.

Awareness helps Heart live with joy and love
in the HERE and NOW.

3

AWARENESS

4

Awareness is a tool we use to understand Mind and Heart.

It's like a light that helps us see what is real.

When Awareness is with Heart and Mind, life is not so scary.

5

The friends decide to
paint a picture.

While Heart looks for
the fluffiest cloud to paint,
Mind squeezes out the colors.
And their new friend, Awareness,
shines its light on them.
They make the perfect team.

Painting feels so fun! I love being outside.
The clouds are beautiful. More paint, please!

I have to do a really good job, but this is so hard.
I give up! I'm not good at painting!

Mind can't hear you, Heart,
because there are stormy clouds
blocking your voice.

Clouds?
You mean the ones in the sky?

9

No, these clouds are filled with words,
feelings, and memories.
They make Mind feel scared,
angry, sad, and hurt.

When there are lots of clouds,
it's hard to hear Heart's voice.

The good news is that I can help Mind
move the stormy clouds away by shining my light.
Soon, they will disappear.

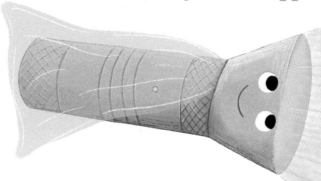

And then I can tell Mind to breathe!
Breathing helps Mind to stop worrying about
yesterday or tomorrow and instead, be in the
HERE and NOW.

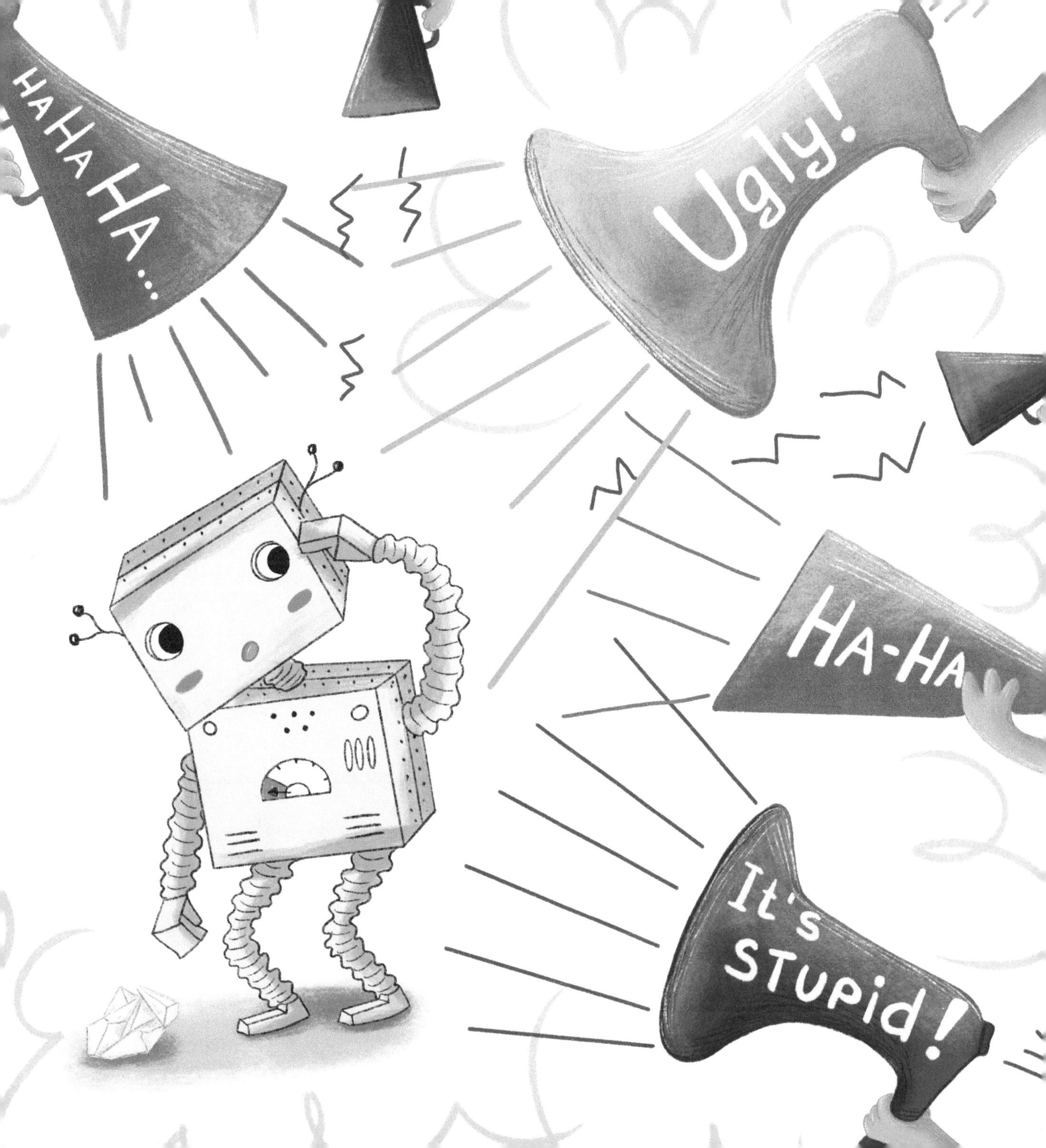

HA HA HA HA...
Ugly!
HA-HA
It's STUPID!

I felt sad because people laughed
at the boat I made yesterday.
I stopped painting because
I was afraid I wouldn't do a good job.

It's okay, Mind. I'm always here loving you,
even when you feel are feeling sad or afraid.

When I shine my light
you can see that
everything will be okay.

The heavy thoughts and feelings
might come back but they will pass.

They are like clouds that come and go
and sometimes block the sun.

But with our help, they won't stay for long.

Mind knows that if the clouds come back,
Heart and Awareness are always by its side.

That's what friends are for.

WELL-BEING EXERCISES

AWARENESS HELPS US SEE THAT LIFE IS NOT SO SCARY

✿ When it is dark in your room, how does it feel to look under your bed?

✿ Now, turn the light on. How does it feel now?

✿ How can you use awareness in other areas that feel scary?

IF YOU'RE UNABLE TO FEEL YOUR HEART'S LOVE AND JOY, THERE ARE STORMY CLOUDS AROUND

✿ Lie down and place your hand over your heart. Can you feel your heartbeat?

✿ Now, place pillows on your chest. Can you feel your heartbeat?

✿ The pillows are like the stormy clouds or emotions that are heavy and make it hard for you to hear your heart. The next time you don't feel love or joy, release the stormy clouds by following the steps below.

HOW TO RELEASE A STORMY CLOUD

✿ Close your eyes.

✿ Breathe in and breathe out.

✿ Bring your attention to your body.

✿ Where is the stormy cloud? In your belly? Throat? Head? Legs?

🌼 Place a pillow or stuffed animal on the spot
where you feel the heavy cloud.

🌼 What does the stormy cloud feel like? Mad? Sad? Hurt?

🌼 Focus your awareness (turn your flashlight on)
on the pillow or stuffed animal and keep breathing.

🌼 Keep going until the stormy cloud has floated away!

AFTER THE STORMY CLOUD HAS PASSED

🌼 What did the stormy cloud feel like?

🌼 What happened when it went away?

🌼 Do you think it might come back?

🌼 Draw a picture of the stormy cloud.

FEELINGS COME AND GO, JUST LIKE THE CLOUDS

🌼 Pick your favorite yoga pose: down dog, tree, butterfly, cow, or touch your toes.

🌼 Stay in the pose for one minute.

🌼 As tiredness or discomfort shows up in your arms and legs,
stay with it and breathe.

🌼 When the time is up, slowly leave the pose.

🌼 What did you learn about tiredness and discomfort?
Did they stay for long? Or did they float away just like a cloud?

Email hello@joyparade.co for more ideas about how your child can release stormy clouds.

Hello, Caregivers!

The goal of this book is to introduce to children the concept of awareness and how it can be used in everyday life.

Awareness helps us understand and neutralize situations, allowing them to feel less personal. Unconscious patterns like bullying, judgment, and anger become conscious as our awareness grows. As the saying goes, "hurt people hurt people." When awareness grows, and we become conscious of our emotions, we are more able to transcend behaviors that cause us (or others) to be hurt.

Another word for awareness is presence. Heavy emotions (stormy clouds) come and go, and becoming more aware or present will help the emotions pass without allowing children to label themselves as the manifested emotion (e.g. "I am an angry person"). Additionally, they will realize that even when experiencing a heavy emotion, they are still loved by their own heart, and by others, leading to increased emotional resilience. They will still be okay during and after a major emotional storm.

As kids are learning how to function in this world, the best gift we can give them is the space to be, especially when they are feeling anger, grief, or rejection. When we can be completely present with them, it helps children see that there isn't anything wrong with having an emotion. When we don't react personally to their storm, they will learn that they can remain aware of the emotion on a feeling level (Where is the feeling? What does it feel like?) before it turns into anxious thinking. It's the emotion that feels scariest to the child and to us. Our awareness can help us see that there is nothing to be afraid of and nothing wrong with us for experiencing these feelings.

I hope you and your loved ones have enjoyed this second book in my series! They help spread the message that feelings are not bad; you are allowed to feel them fully; and they will eventually always pass. With or without a heavy emotion, you are unconditionally loved, always.

Love,
Nishi

ABOUT THE AUTHOR

NISHI SINGHAL has a bachelor's degree in psychology from the University of Michigan and a master's degree in public health from the University of Illinois of Chicago. For over ten years, Nishi has worked with various nonprofits with the goal of bettering communities. She is currently the director of the Lively Community Foundation, an organization dedicated to uplifting wellness in the world

Inspired by her work with children through teaching yoga, Nishi created Joy Parade, an online space dedicated to teaching children and their caregivers how to bring presence into their day-to-day living. Nishi wrote *A Friendship Story: Heart & Mind* to teach presence to children so they can live a more balanced and joyful life. Her second book, *Heart & Mind: Meet a New Friend,* focuses on helping children release heavy emotions by becoming more aware of their feelings.

Visit JoyParade.co to learn more.

ABOUT THE ILLUSTRATOR

LERA MUNOZ is an illustrator specializing in children's illustration. She loves to create playful characters and imaginary worlds that inspire young minds. Her work is perfect for storytelling and has been described as "charming and full of warmth."

Lera lives in France with her husband and 5-year old daughter. Being from Russia and now living in France, Lera takes the best from both cultures. In her free time, she likes to read, meditate, and travel. Life is filled with domestic warmth and smiles of family and friends.

Visit leramunoz.com.

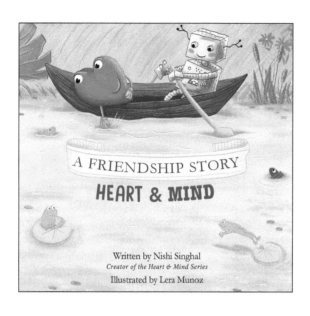

A FRIENDSHIP STORY: HEART & MIND

Come along with the very best friends, Heart & Mind, as they work together to keep each other balanced. Heart brings in joy and love in the present moment, while Mind takes action. But what happens when they spend the day apart? This is a story to remind your child of the importance of listening to their heart and taking positive action, leading to a more joyous life!

TESTIMONIALS

This is a beautiful book. The words and ideas are clear. The content is understandable for both young and older elementary children. There are educational extensions easily accessible for both teachers and parents.

~**BARBARA KILLIAN,** Grandmother &
Retired Elementary School Special Needs Teacher

When our children understand the inner workings of their heart and mind, they can find their own peace. What greater gift to give our children than the gift of peace?

~**FELICITY POWERS**, Middle School Teacher and Therapist

Beyond impressed with how Nishi broke down concepts that many adults have a hard time with, for kids!

~**JESS LIVELY**, Host of The Lively Show Podcast

CPSIA information can be obtained
at www.ICGtesting.com
Printed in the USA
BVHW021954190821
614611BV00035B/1229